# MANET
## A NEW REALISM

*BY*

DAVID SPENCE

# THE WORLD IN THE 1860'S

*'We have all of us got the republican spirit in our veins, as we have the pox in our bones'* - *Charles Baudelaire*. Baudelaire, the French poet, critic and friend of Edouard Manet, was convinced that art should be about *la vie moderne* (modern life) not mythology or history. Art should be rooted in reality, the reality of modern man who fought in the Paris revolution in 1848; who worked in the factories of the great industrial nations such as England, France and Germany; who built the railways and ships that were expanding the wealth of trading nations around the world; who fought in America for the right to be free from slavery. He believed that art, like science, should reveal the truth. Art should be a mirror held up to the world, showing men and women as they really were, the beggar, the alcoholic, the shop girl, the prostitute. Artists such as Courbet and Manet were searching for a new realism, seeking to represent the 'heroism of modern life'.

## EVOLUTION

Charles Darwin wrote a book that shocked the world when it was published in 1859. The book was called *On the Origin of Species* and attempted to explain that humans were related to animals through a process of evolution, or unfolding, as gradually over millions of years animals adapted to better suit the conditions in which they lived.

President Lincoln's Union army fought for the abolition of slavery which still kept millions of African Americans in forced labour. The North was victorious and the war over by April 1865. Despite the abolition of slavery, most slaves could not integrate into a society which still did not tolerate them

## THE TRADE CANAL

The Suez Canal cuts through 100 miles of Egyptian mainland linking the Mediterranean Sea and the Red Sea. It took ten years to build with French help and opened in 1869. The canal enabled shipping to avoid the long journey south around the African continent, cutting over 7,000 miles from the distance that ships needed to sail to reach the Far East.

## THE REVOLUTIONARY THINKER

Exiled from his home country of Germany, Karl Marx moved to England in 1849 where he developed his ideas about the economics of capitalism and class struggle. In 1867 his theories were published in a book entitled *Das Kapital* which was to become the communist 'bible'. Marx believed that the struggle between the rich rulers and the poor workers would result in revolution, and that the workers would overthrow their masters: *'the workers have nothing to lose but their chains'*. Marx died in London in 1883.

In 1917 the Russian revolution established the first communist state based on his ideas.

## FREE TRADE?

Western European powers had forced the unwilling Chinese to open their frontiers to trade in the 1840's. After the seizure of a British ship and the murder of a missionary an armed Anglo-French expedition was sent to bombard Canton in retaliation. Armed skirmishes continued as the Chinese continued to resist the European imperial presence and in 1859 the British burned the Chinese Imperial Summer Palace. This pressure eventually forced China to sign a treaty opening up eleven Chinese ports to foreign trade.

## FIGHTING FOR FREEDOM

The United States of America was rapidly expanding throughout the nineteenth century. In 1845 Texas joined the Union; in 1848 California was added and European immigrants swelled the population to ever higher numbers. In 1860 Abraham Lincoln was elected president, prompting the state of South Carolina to declare independence. The following year more Southern states left the Union and civil war erupted between the Northern Union and the Confederacy of the Southern states.

# THE WORLD OF MANET

**EDOUARD MANET**

Edouard Manet was born in Paris on 23 January 1832, the eldest of three sons born to Auguste Manet and Eugenie Desiree Fournier. Edouard was urged by his father to take up a career in the legal profession but his interests were in art, not law. Art was not an acceptable career as far as Auguste Manet was concerned; instead Edouard applied to join the naval college, but failed the entrance examination. He then joined the Merchant Marine and in 1848 set sail on the training ship *Le Havre et Guadeloupe,* bound for Brazil. Manet describes the journey in detail in his letters home. He was shocked at what he saw in Rio de Janeiro. '*In this country all the negroes are slaves, they all look downtrodden; it's extraordinary what power the whites have over them; I saw a slave market, a rather revolting spectacle for people like us*'. France had abolished slavery in its Caribbean colonies as recently as March of the previous year.

When the young Manet arrived back in France in 1849 he was determined to become an artist and his father relented, allowing him to enrol at the studio of the artist Thomas Couture in Paris. Manet was to enjoy the life of the Parisian *flaneur* (stroller). This meant a person of sophistication and elegance, a dandy with white gloves, top hat and cane, who strolled the boulevards and mixed with the bohemian painters, writers and composers in the many fashionable cafes. The word *rentier* also applied to Manet. This meant a person of private financial means who was free, as Manet was, to indulge in his desires rather than needing to work for his living.

**BRAZILIAN SCENES**

Manet felt no embarrassment in communicating his feelings about the Brazilian peoples and their habits. In a letter to his mother Manet writes '*most Brazilian women are very pretty: they have superb dark eyes and hair to match... they never go out alone but are always followed by their black maid or accompanied by their children... The Carnival of Rio is something quite special... At 3 o'clock all the Brazilian ladies are at their front doors or on their balconies, bombarding every gentleman who passes by with multicoloured wax balls filled with water; these are called limons. My pockets were filled with limons and I gave as good as I got, which is the proper thing to do*'.

## THE BARRICADE, 1871

*Manet's Observation of the Streets of Paris*

It was clear from letters home from Brazil in 1848 that Manet was a republican. On that occasion he wrote to his father '*Try to keep for our return a healthy Republic.*' When France made the disastrous move of declaring war on Prussia in 1870 the French army was quickly over-run and Paris was under siege. Manet joined the National Guard. He recorded: '*We're beginning to feel the pinch here, horsemeat is a delicacy, donkey is exorbitantly expensive, there are butcher's shops for dogs, cats and rats...*' But worse was to follow. The defeat led to conflict between the Parisian National Guard and the army resulting in civil war. The suppression of the Paris Commune in 1871 led to the death of over 20,000 Communards. The English journalist Archibald Forbes wrote '*Europe professes civilization and France boasts of culture and Frenchmen are braining one another with the butt end of muskets, and Paris is burning*'.

## BULLFIGHT, 1865/66

Manet visited Madrid in 1865 and fell under the spell of Spanish painting. The work of Spanish artists such as Velazquez and Goya had a profound influence on Manet's own style of painting and choice of subject matter. *Spanish fashion* was very popular in Paris at this time with the Louvre art gallery acquiring works by Spanish artists and popular entertainment such as the Ambassadeurs Theatre playing Spanish dance troupes nightly. Manet developed this picture from the sketches he made while attending bullfights in Spain.

## ROMANS OF THE DECADENCE

### Thomas Couture

The teaching of art in France was the responsibility of the Ecoles des Beaux-Arts. The Ecoles (schools) taught according to principles set by the Academies almost 200 years earlier: Academies existed to preserve traditions, not to create new ones.

The Romanticism of Delacroix had begun to shake the foundations of the establishment of the Academies; their view of classical art as representing the image of moral beauty physical perfection, and as a means of redirecting the mind to purer things was becoming outdated. Man did not want to study at the Ecoles. Instead he paid 120 francs a year for tuition from Thomas Couture wh was an artist with an excellent reputation whose classical subjects were painted with a modern touc

Fantin-Latour, Champfleury, Manet, Baudelaire.
Alphonse Legros, Felix Bracquemand and Edmond Duranty are also shown but not identified.

## HOMAGE TO DELACROIX

### Henri Fantin-Latour

The artistic and literary set that Manet mixed with in Paris are represented in this painting by Henri Fantin-Latour. It is called *Homage to Delacroix* because Delacroix's portrait is shown in the cent of the painting. Delacroix ha said that if an artist lacked th skill to draw a man falling o of a fifth floor window in th time it takes for him to hit the ground he would never produce a 'monumental' wo Critics have pointed out, however, that none of those depicted is actually looking the portrait of Delacroix. Th critic Jean Rousseau express the view that the painting w devoted to the *glory of realis*

## THE BIRTH OF VENUS

### Alexandre Cabanel

It was every artist's ambition to have his work exhibited in the *Salon* in Paris. The female nude was a popular subject, particularly when it was represented in an acceptable way such as Cabanel's painting of the Venus creation myth, despite its overt eroticism. The *Salon* was crucial to an artist because there was no real alternative place of exhibition for an artist's work.

# THE ART OF HIS DAY

French art in the first half of the 19th century had been dominated by the Romantic painter Eugene Delacroix who had turned to contemporary and exotic literary references, such as Byron, for subject matter instead of the classical approach favoured by French academicians. The artist Gustave Courbet rejected any notion of idealization in art, rejecting both classicism and romanticism in favour of a natural representation of everyday life. Courbet stated that only realism was really democratic and that the noblest subject for the artist to paint was the peasant and worker. Manet's own particular style took on board the influence of Spanish art and Impressionist technique but owed much to Courbet's dedication to realism.

THE BARGE
(MONET PAINTING ON HIS
STUDIO BOAT), 1874 (detail)

Monet was influenced and encouraged by Manet who introduced him to the artistic circles in Paris. Monet recalled that in 1869 Manet invited him to a cafe in the Batignolles area where he and his friends met every evening after leaving their studios. Some years later Monet was to persuade Manet to work *en plein air* painting out of doors in the 'fresh air' instead of in his studio.

## THE PAINTER'S STUDIO

*Gustave Courbet*

This monumental picture has a title to match, *The Painter's Studio: A Real Allegory Summing up Seven Years of My Artistic Life.* It was painted by Courbet in 1855, at the height of his fame. The figures in the painting are about life size, so big is the canvas, and represent specific people and types. Courbet's friends such as Baudelaire and the Realist writer Champfleury are included along with allegorical figures such as truth (the naked woman is the naked truth, meaning art should be true to life) and the untutored, innocent eyes of youth examining Courbet's landscape.

**PORTRAIT OF MONSIEUR AND MADAME MANET, 1860**

A few days after the birth of his son Auguste Manet was named a Chevalier of the Legion of Honour. This honour, along with the birth of a son, must have brought happiness to the Manet household. The following year a second son was born and named Eugene. Two years later a third son, Gustave, was born to the Manets. Eugenie was 20 years old when she married Auguste, 14 years younger than her husband. In 1857, three years before this portrait was painted, Auguste was stricken with paralysis. He was unable to use his legs for over a year and he lost the power of speech, causing him to resign from his post of judge at the Court of the First Instance. Auguste died in 1862 but Eugenie was to outlive her eldest son by two years.

# FAMILY, FRIENDS & OTHERS

Edouard Manet was born on 23 January 1832 into a prosperous middle class family who were university educated land owners. His father, Auguste Manet, followed his own father's footsteps into a career as a magistrate and judge and expected his first born son Edouard to do the same. The Manets were the very picture of respectability, a model Parisian family. Manet's mother, Eugenie Desiree, was the goddaughter of the Crown Prince of Sweden. She brought with her a considerable dowry as well as perhaps even

greater social standing. The family lived in an imposing four storey apartment house at 5, rue Bonapart near the Seine. Manet attended Cano Poiloup's school when he was six years old, moving on to the College Rollin, a boarding school, at twelve.

## FRIENDS IN HIGH PLACES

Manet and Antonin Proust became friends when they met at school. Prou studied painting with Manet at Couture's studio before he decided to become a journalist. They remained lifelong friends. Manet painted th portrait in 1880 when Proust had been appointed Minister of Fine A *Portrait of Antonin Proust, 1877 (detail).*

## LEON THE UNRECOGNIZED SON

Was Leon the illegitimate son of Edouard Manet? All the evidence suggests that this is the case although some think that he might have been Auguste Manet's son rather than Edouard's. It is difficult to believe, however, that Manet would have lived with and later married the mother of his father's son. Manet rented an apartment for Suzanne and Leon until their marriage, after which they lived together. For the sake of appearances and fear of becoming social outcasts Suzanne never outwardly recognised Leon as her son, and it seems that he was unaware that his own name and parentage were false until he was 20 years old. When Manet died he specified in his will that his estate should pass to his wife Suzanne, and thence to Leon. In 1900, a year before her death, Suzanne finally recognized Leon as her son so that he might benefit from her inheritance. Even then she never made public the name of Leon's father.

~1832~
Edouard Manet born
on 23 January

~1848~
Manet joined the
Merchant Marine and
went to Brazil

~1849~
Returned to Paris and
enrolled at
the studio of
Thomas Couture.
Met Suzanne Leenhoff

~1852~
Leon Edouard born
on 29 January

~1862~
Manet's father died.
Met Victorine Meurent

## SUZANNE READING

Suzanne Leenhoff had moved from her native town of Zaltbommel in Holland to Paris at the early age of 19, making her living as a piano teacher. In 1849 the seventeen year old Manet met Suzanne when she was hired by Manet's mother to teach her sons to play the piano. At some point they became lovers after which Suzanne hurriedly disappeared to Holland. She later returned having given birth to a son named Leon Edouard, who was born on January 29 1852, almost 20 years to the day after the birth of Edouard. An illegitimate child was unacceptable to a family of Manet's standing so Leon was passed off as Manet's godson and younger brother of Suzanne. When Suzanne returned she lived with her grandmother, son Leon, and two younger brothers, almost certainly with the financial support of the Manet family. Suzanne and Manet were not married until 1863, the year following the death of Manet's father.

This portrait of Suzanne was begun 1865, when she was 35 years old. It is painted in cool greys and whites but is nevertheless a tender and affectionate portrayal. The figure standing behind Suzanne reading from a book is her son, Leon. He was added to the painting several years later which explains why he looks older than he should have been at the time the painting was made.

# THE LIFE OF MANET

~1863~
Manet and Suzanne Leenhoff are married.
*Le Dejeuner sur l'Herbe* exhibited

~1865~
Visited Madrid and saw paintings by Velazquez and Goya.
*Olympia* exhibited

~1867~
Execution of Maximilian, Emperor of Mexico.
Manet holds his own exhibition on Avenue Montaigne

~1868~
Met Berthe Morisot

~1869~
Manet invited Claude Monet to a cafe to meet fellow artists

~1870~
France declared war on Prussia

~1871~
The Paris Commune defeated

~1873~
Met Stephen Mallarme

~1881~
*A Bar at the Folies Bergere* exhibited

~1883~
Death of Manet on 30 April

~1901~
Death of Suzanne Leenhoff

## PORTRAIT OF STEPHEN MALLARME, 1876

Manet met Mallarme, an English teacher, in October 1873. Mallarme taught at a school near the Gare Saint Lazare and lived on the rue de Moscou, not far from Manet's studio on the rue de Saint Petersbourg. Mallarme was already having some success as a poet when Manet first knew him and the two became close friends. Manet illustrated some of Mallarme publications, including his translation of Edgar Allan Poe's *The Raven*. In 1881 Manet wrote to Mallarme '*I feel very guilty and am afraid yo may be a bit cross with me, because I've been thinking, after all, it's selfish of n not to have accepted the work you proposed - but it's also true that some of th things you suggested seem impossible, such as the woman lying in bed, see through a window. You are a terrible lot, you poets, and it's often impossible visualize the things you imagine*'

## BERTHE MORISOT WITH BLACK HAT AND VIOLETS, 1872

Berthe Morisot and her sister Edma were determined to become artists and had persuaded their mother to let them take art lessons. Women artists were frowned upon in Manet's day, particularly women from the Morisots' social background. The teacher warned Berthe and Edma's mother '*They will become painters; do you realize what this means? In your upper class milieu this would be a revolution, I would almost say a catastrophe*'. Manet met the Morisots in 1868. Berthe Morisot and Manet became good friends, perhaps even lovers, but there is no evidence for this other than the intimacy of Manet's portrait of Berthe and the intensity of thei relationship. Man kept in his stud five out of th eleven portrai he painted of Berthe

# A SPECIAL FRIEND

**M**anet's friends, many of whom are now familiar names, mixed in the artistic and literary circles which inhabited the sophisticated cafe life of Paris. Manet would sit long into the evening discussing art with the younger painters who looked up to him as leader of the revolt against the old values of the French art world. Artists such as Claude Monet, Alfred Sisley, and Auguste Renoir who were to lead the Impressionist revolution received Manet's support although he was careful not to include himself in their Impressionist group. Though he was happy to play the part of modern master Manet did in fact care for and sought approval from the traditional art establishment. He desperately wanted his paintings to be accepted by the *Salon* and be met with critical acclaim.

### THE BALCONY, 1868/69

During 1868 Manet started work on a group portrait entitled *The Balcony*. It was exhibited at the *Salon* in 1869, receiving the usual critical response, one caricature was accompanied by the words '*Do close that window, M Manet, what I am telling you is for your own good*'. The painting concentrates very much on the seated figure of Berthe Morisot whose intent black eyes stare out of the picture. Manet had only recently met Berthe and her sister Edma but this picture shows his fascination for her. In comparison the figure of Fanny Claus who stands next to her is hardly finished. In the background stands Manet's friend Antoine Guillemet, and intriguingly just visible in the shadows is the face of Manet's son, Leon. Berthe went to the *Salon* to view the painting and found Manet '*with his hat over his eyes, looking bewildered, he begged me to look at the painting since he did not dare to himself... He laughed uneasily, declaring at one and the same time that his painting was very bad and that it would be very successful*'.

### BERTHE MORISOT

Berthe Morisot broke the conventions and became a successful artist. She was invited to join the Impressionist group by Degas in recognition of her work. This may have been a difficult decision because Manet had already turned down a similar invitation but in 1874 she did join the group and exhibited at the independent Impressionist exhibition.

This may have been a deliberate act to distance herself from the overpowering influence of Manet and assert herself as an independent artist. In December 1874 Berthe married Manet's brother, Eugene, who resembled Manet in many ways. Manet and Berthe continued to be close friends, sharing their passion for painting.

*A Young Woman* by Berthe Morisot *(detail)*

# THE MODEL ARTIST

*M*anet's favourite model was Victorine Meurent. Victorine was a native Parisian from a poor family who would have had little opportunity to mix with the likes of Manet other than as an artist's model or perhaps as a prostitute. It was a fact of life in the 1860's that men such as Manet did not encounter women such as Victorine in any social sense. We know that she had worked as an artist's model for Manet's art teacher, Thomas Couture (after Manet had left the studio) as well as for other artists, and that Manet met her in 1862 when she was 18 years old – '*by chance in a crowd… and had been struck by her original and distinctive appearance*' – according to Manet's friend, Theodore Duret. Victorine was an artist in her own right, exhibiting a self-portrait at the *Salon* in 1876. Ironically, Manet's work was refused by the *Salon* that year.

## PORTRAIT OF VICTORINE MEURENT

Victorine was 18 when Manet painted this portrait in 1862. She was to model for Manet on and off for the next 13 years, appearing in different guises in many of his best known paintings. It is likely that they were lovers; certainly Manet's marriage would have been no obstacle for a man of his social position provided it was a private rather than a public affair. Victorine had striking red hair and a fair complexion. From examination of the preparatory studies of both *Le Dejeuner sur l'Herbe* (page 14/15) and *Olympia* (page 18) it is obvious that Victorine was the model, even though Manet darkened the hair colouring in the final version of both paintings.

What is important about Manet's relationship with Victorine, however, is that in her face he found 'truth'. Manet said many times that his mission was to paint 'the real truth'. The portrait of Victorine shows an attractive redhead with creamy skin and light eyelashes, but she is not made to look pretty, nor is she idealised. It was Victorine's face that was so 'real', literally the kind of woman you saw on the streets of Paris, that made it so shocking when Manet depicted it in paintings such as *Olympia*.

*The Street Singer,* 1862 *(detail)*

## CHERRI

In this picture Victorine portrayed a street singer, holding some fres looking cherries wrapped brown pap

## THE FACE FROM
### *LE DEJEUNER SUR L'HERBE*

As far as the art-going public were concerned, a painting of a naked goddess was acceptable, even if the model was the artist's mistress (so long as she was not recognisable), but a real woman painted without clothes was not a 'decent' woman because what decent woman would let herself be seen without clothes? Manet broke the rules in the name of truth and modernity.

Victorine had to suffer the scorn of the public and accusations of the press, which she did with fortitude.

## THE FACE FROM
### *GARE SAINT-LAZARE*

Victorine had travelled to America but in 1873 she returned, and Manet took the opportunity once more to include her in a painting. This is very different from the earlier pictures for which Victorine posed; she now wears a distant look, the book and dog sleeping on her lap tell of a more settled life, probably reflecting the cooling effect of time and separation on their relationship.

## VICTORINE AS *OLYMPIA*

After Manet's death Victorine wrote to his widow, Suzanne, asking for money '*You doubtless know that I posed for a large portion of his paintings, notably Olympia, his masterpiece. M Manet was concerned about me and often said that if he sold his pictures he would set aside a gratuity for me, I was young then, and carefree. I left for America. When I returned, M Manet, who had sold a large number of pictures… told me that a share of that was mine. I refused… and added that when I could no longer pose I would remind him of that promise. That time has come sooner than I expected*'. Victorine is reported to have taken to drink, and disappeared from the scene.

# WHAT DO THE PAINTINGS SAY?

*M*anet's good friend and fellow student Antonin Proust has described the moment when Manet decided to make the painting which was to become *Le Dejeuner sur l'Herbe*. According to Proust, while sitting on the banks of the Seine at the Paris suburb of Argenteuil, Manet's attention was caught by some bathers. Manet then said to Proust '*I'm told that I must do a nude. All right, I will. I'll do them a nude. Back in our student days, I copied Giorgione's women, the women with the musicians. That's a dark picture. The background has retreated. I'm going to do it over, and do it in the transparency of the atmosphere, with figures like you see over there*'. Manet's picture does refer back to earlier work by great Italian masters such as Titian (Manet referred to a painting which has since been attributed to Titian rather than Giorgione). He wanted to incorporate references to art of an earlier period to demonstrate not just his learning but that tradition can extend into modern 'realist' painting.

## MANET'S FAVOURITE

The model for the naked woman who looks at the viewer so directly and without a trace of shame was Victorine Meurent, a professional model whom Manet first met in 1862, the year before the picture was made. Victorine would have been 19 years old at the time, and had already been the subject of many of Manet's paintings. A preparatory study for the painting shows the female figure with red hair, the colour of Victorine's own hair, but Manet has changed it to brown for the final version.

## HUMOROUS FROG

The inclusion of a frog may have been a reference to *grenouille*; the French word for frog was also the slang word for prostitute.

## HIDDEN SIGNS

Manet clearly made art historical references to more than just the Raphael picture. The overturned basket was a symbol of the loss of innocence, fruits such as peaches, cherries and figs were also recognised symbols and the empty oyster shells signal that the oysters, always regarded as an aphrodisiac, have already been consumed

## IN THE FAMILY

The male figure at the centre of the picture was based on Ferdinand Leenhoff, brother of Suzanne Leenhoff who became Manet's wife. The figure on the right was that of Manet's brother Eugene, who posed for the painting.

## SCANDAL AT THE SALON

*Le Dejeuner sur l'Herbe* was exhibited in 1863 at the *Salon des Refuses*, the alternative exhibition to the official *Salon,* and caused an immediate outcry. Manet's picture quickly became the *succes de scandale*; why was the woman naked but the men clothed? This was apparently a modern painting depicting a real event with men in Parisian dress having luncheon on the grass *(Dejeuner sur l'Herbe)*. Such a scene would have been acceptable if it were cloaked in the respectability of the classical tradition (not in modern dress!), but Manet had flaunted tradition by painting real people in a modern world. The critic Ernest Chesneau attacked the painting accusing Manet of trying to attain celebrity by shocking the bourgeois. Manet replied by saying that he obviously should have painted the men in the nude as well as the woman, as they would be in an old master painting. Nevertheless Manet did become a celebrity as a result of the picture.

## JUDGEMENT OF PARIS

*Marcantonio Raimondi*

This engraving by Raimondi, after the painting by Raphael dating from around 1520, clearly shows the inspiration for the three seated figures in Manet's painting. The nakedness of the

River Gods in this classical image did not offend, but Manet's version angered the critics and public alike. The critics were quick to pick up the 'art historical' reference which Manet enjoyed making.

## VIVA MEXICO

The shirt worn by Maximilian at his execution was removed and photographed. It shows the bullet holes which dealt him the final blow as he shouted '*Viva Mexico!*'

After the execution Maximilian's body was displayed in his coffin with black marbles replacing his eyes.

# WHAT DO THE PAINTINGS SAY?

The French were the greatest foreign influence on Mexico in the 1860's. In 1863 French troops installed the Austrian Archduke Maximilian as Emperor of Mexico, following a suppression of the revolutionary republican government of Benito Juarez which refused to recognize Mexico's debts to France, Britain and Spain. The French thought Mexico held great mineral wealth and grimly hung on to power fearful of American expansion. Emperor Napoleon III of France hoped to forge an alliance with Austria and to retain control over Mexico by promising the young Archduke Ferdinand 33,000 French troops to support him. At the end of the American civil war i 1865 American aid supported the ousted Juarez; at the same time Napoleon thought twice about Austria's value as an ally after it had been defeated by the Prussia army. Napoleon decided to cut his losses and withdrew hi troops from Mexico, leaving the hapless Archduke Maximilian at the mercy of Juarez's army.

### THE THIRD OF MAY

*Francisco Goya*

This painting which illustrates the atrocities committed by the French against the Spanish was made by Goya in 1808. Manet would certainly have seen it when he visited Madrid in 1865, just two years before he painted the Execution of Maximilian. The similarities are striking, especially the proximity of the soldiers levelling their rifles at the victim who is at the point of death. Both Goya and Manet position the victims with arms outstretched in a Christ-like pose.

## THE EXECUTION OF MAXIMILIAN

Maximilian refused to bow to Juarez's demands that he abdicate power and return home. He mistakenly believed that Europe would come to his aid and sent his wife to Paris to summon help. However Juarez had passed a law which stated that anyone who helped foreign intervention in Mexico should face the death penalty. Maximilian was duly executed by firing squad alongside his two generals, Miramon and Mejia. In July 1867 the first news of the execution was reported in France in *Le Figaro*. Manet fell upon the subject with enthusiasm, and made several paintings on the execution theme. As more news reports of the event came back to France so Manet made changes to his pictures to suit.

### FOUR PAINTINGS

Manet painted four versions of the event. The first shows the firing squad dressed in Mexican uniform, in the last version (shown here) the uniforms resemble those of the French Imperial Guard Light Infantry, serving to illustrate how the public perception of blame had shifted from Juarez to Napoleon. The sheer brutality of the scene is conveyed in an almost journalistic way by Manet. Photographs of the incident were suppressed but verbal accounts circulated widely in the press and it is almost as if Manet illustrates the verbal accounts as a photograph might have done.

The second version was cut up by Leon, Manet's son, after the artist's death. Leon considered only a part of the picture good enough to sell (the sergeant examining his rifle), which he sold to Degas. Although interest from buyers persuaded Leon to recover and sell other portions of the picture some had gone forever, apparently used by Leon to light a fire.

...aximilian stands ...n the centre, ...ring a sombrero, ...e soldiers fire at ...t blank range at his general.

### ENTRY OF NAPOLEON III INTO PARIS ON 2 DECEMBER 1852

Louis Napoleon Bonaparte became president of the Second Republic of France. His actions over the Maximilian affair brought disgrace followed in 1870 by the collapse of the Empire.

The soldier at the rear who appears to be casually examining his rifle is preparing to perform the *coup de grace*.

### THE REAL OLYMPIA

What made matters worse as far as the critics were concerned was the fact th
the real identity of *Olympia* was well known: it was Manet's favourite model,
Victorine Meurent. As with *Le Dejeuner sur l'Herbe* the earlier studies for
*Olympia* show quite clearly the features and red hair of Victorine. In the final
painting the courtesan's hair has been toned down to dark brown.

### OLYMPIA, 1863

So why were
people so shocked by
Manet's painting? The naked
female had been painted time and again
throughout the history of art and certainly
was not unusual. What made Manet's
*Olympia* different? She did not conform
to the stereotype of the nude in art which
cast women as anonymous mythical
figures, handmaidens and nymphs. Manet's
woman is recognizably real, a modern
prostitute who looks out at the spectator
in a matter of fact way directly and
intimately involving the spectator in
the scene, and by doing so places the
spectator in the role of client. The critics
and public reacted violently because
they felt intimidated, even violated by
*Olympia*. The critic who warned young
girls and pregnant women to flee was
admitting that he could not reconcile his
own view of the woman's role in the
boudoir with her role in the family.

### A SELF POSSESSED LADY

We are not invited to stare at *Olympia's* nakedness as p
of some remote scene from a made-up history, there
no excuse or pretence for her nakedness, instead we
are confronted with a modern day courtesan who is
unashamed and self possessed, aware of the power of h
body. The critics could not mask their recognition o
*Olympia* from their own experiences, and were angr
that the real world had invaded the safe world of art

### VENUS OF URBINO *Titian*

It cannot escape notice that Manet based the
composition of his painting on Titian's *Venus of Urbino,
1538*. It is known that Manet had seen and made a copy
of Titian's painting on an earlier trip to Italy. Titian's *Venus*
shows a seductive female who looks enticingly at the
spectator, but is quite passive compared to *Olympia*.

### VENUS'S DOG

At the feet of Titia
Venus lies a dog
curled up and fast
asleep. The dog is a
well known symbol
which artists use to
represent faithfulness and
adds a powerful message to this painting
about the behaviour of Venus.

# WHAT DO THE PAINTINGS SAY?

Manet painted *Olympia* in 1863, the same year as *Le Dejeuner sur l'Herbe*, but did not submit it for exhibition at the *Salon* until 1865. He was undoubtedly worried about the reaction of the critics but it seemed that his friend Charles Baudelaire persuaded him to put the painting forward. Manet's fears were confirmed. The critics and public alike were baffled and outraged by *Olympia*. One critic said '*I do not know whether the dictionary of French aesthetics holds expressions to characterize her... her face is stupid, her skin cadaverous*'. He referred to Manet as '*a brute who paints green women with dish brushes*' and furthermore advised young girls and pregnant women to flee *this spectacle*. A review of the painting in *L'Artiste* continues '*What is this Odalisque with a yellow stomach? A base model picked up I know not where, who represents Olympia? Olympia? What Olympia? A courtesan no doubt*'. Manet was shattered by the criticism. He later recalled that '*The attacks directed against me broke me in the mainspring of life. No one knows what it is to be constantly insulted. It disheartens you and undoes you*'.

## YMPIA'S CAT

contrast to he faithful og Manet ncludes a ack cat at mpia's feet. e cat is the pposite of us's dog. The at represents promiscuous haviour, even the ng word for cat – *otte* – also meant stitute. The black became associated th Manet's name for many years ter the painting was exhibited.

NANA, 1877 *(detail)*

Views did not change over time. In 1877 Manet submitted this painting to the *Salon* which rejected it as 'immoral'. The subject is clearly a courtesan, and was based on the actress Henrietta Hauser, an acquaintance of Manet. Manet's friend, the writer Emile Zola, had a book published in 1880 entitled *Nana* which continued the theme of prostitution.

# HOW WERE THEY MADE?

*M*anet started out working in the traditional manner of the studio based artist, making sketches and notes for paintings which were worked on in carefully controlled circumstances in his studio on the rue de Douai. The influences of the great French masters such as Delacroix and Ingres as well as his favourite Spanish artists contributed to his unique style which appeared more and more to highlight his subjects against a flat background, as if picked out by a spotlight against a theatre backdrop. Manet never became part of the Impressionist set even though many called him the King of Impressionism and art historians refer to Manet as the 'father' of Impressionism.

Manet's obsession, which was taken even further by the Impressionists, wa to paint only what he saw, what appeared in front of his eyes.

### LINSEED

The seeds of the flax plant yield a yellow oil which has been used as a medium for oil painting for centuries because of its good drying properties.

### OPEN AIR

In 1866 the Impressionist painter Claude Monet painted a picture entitled *Women in the Garden* entirely in the open rather than in his studio. Manet laughed at this *plein air* (open air) method of painting. Although he insisted on realism, this was going too far. After some years however Monet's influence on Manet was apparent and Manet also experimented with *plein air* painting. This was becoming much more practicable with the adver of manufactured paints in tin tubes and portable boxes such as this English example of the late 19th century.

## FRUITS ON A TABLE, 1864

This record of Manet's lesson in still life painting for Eva Gonzales gives a good idea of how Manet went about making a painting. '*Get it down quickly. Don't worry about the background. Just go for the tonal values. You see? When you look at it, and above all when you think how to render it as you see it, that is, in such a way that it makes the same impression on the viewer as it does on you, you don't look for, you don't see the lines on the paper over there do you? And the grapes, now do you count each grape? Of course not. What strikes you is their clear amber colour, and the bloom which models the form by softening it. What you have to decide with the cloth is where the highlights come and then the planes which are not in direct light. Halftones are for the Magasin Pittoresque engravers. The folds will come by themselves if you put them in their proper place*'.

## POPPY SEEDS

During the 19th century experiments with different types of oil media led to the use of oil extracted from poppy seeds. Poppy oil did not yellow as much as other types of oils but was more difficult to extract and therefore more expensive than linseed or walnut oil which was also available. Investigations show that Manet used both poppy and linseed oil.

21

# FAMOUS IMAGES

*I*n March 1863 Manet held an exhibition of his paintings in the gallery of art dealer Louis Martinet on the Boulevard des Italiens, which was an important venue for artists whose work failed to be accepted by the official *Salon*. Among the works to be exhibited was *Music in the Tuileries Gardens*. This was a group portrait of Manet's family and friends and effectively a snapshot of Parisian life. Theodore Duret tells us that '*At that time the Chateau of the Tuileries, where the Emperor held court, was a centre of opulent life which extended to the gardens. The band concerts held there twice a week attracted a sophisticated and elegant crowd*'.

In 1862 Manet went to the gardens almost every day, from two to four, making sketches under the trees, then returned to his studio where he planned and executed the painting. The picture is a snapshot in the photographic sense as well. The framing of the scene with figures cut in half by the edge of the canvas is reminiscent of the way in which the new medium of photography was making 'instant pictures'; the flattened perspective with some areas in focus, some just a blur, also recalls the artlessness of photography.

Charles Baudelaire, poet. One of the most famous of all Manet's friends, and possibly the most influential. A strong advocate of modernity, whose poems shocked as much as Manet's paintings.

Theophile Gautier, art critic.

Henri Fantin-Latour, painter. One of Manet's earliest friends and devoted supporters.

Baron Ta Inspector of Museu

Edouard Manet.

Eugene Manet, the artist's brother.

Albert de Balleroy, with whom Manet shared a studio. He specialized in painting hunting scenes.

Zacharie Astruc, artist, writer and composer. He wrote a poem about Manet's painting *Olympia* as well as collaborating on an illustrated song sheet with Manet.

Madame Loubens.

## MUSIC IN THE TUILERIES GARDENS, 1862

Jacques Offenbach, composer. Internationally renowned for his ght operettas such as *he Tales of Hoffmann*.

Manet would lunch at the Cafe Tortini before making his way to the Tuileries Gardens to sketch. When he had finished, around five or six in the evening, he would return to the Cafe where his artist friends would be waiting to see the results of his work. This admiration was not however shared by the critics and the public. When the painting was exhibited it caused an outrage. One artist, known only as an *amateur* in this account by Emile Zola, was almost moved to violence: '*an exasperated amateur was threatening to take violent action if* Music in the Tuileries *was allowed to remain in the gallery. I understand the anger of the amateur: imagine under the trees of the Tuileries a whole crowd, a hundred people perhaps, who are simply bustling around in the sun; each person is simply a tache, scarcely fixed, on which the details become lines or black dots. If I had been there I would have asked the amateur to stand at a respectful distance: then he would have seen that these taches were alive, that the crowd was talking...*'. The painting includes portraits of many of Manet's family and friends.

### A LITTLE JOKE

Manet played a visual trick on his audience by painting the child's hoop after he had signed the painting. The hoop, which casually leans against a chair, also rests over the top of the artist's name.

Madame Lejosne, wife of Commandant Hippolyte Lejosne in whose home Manet had been introduced to Baudelaire. He had strong Republican sympathies as well as being a supporter of the arts.

## THE TRAPEZE ARTIST

In the very top left hand corner of the painting Manet has painted in a pair of legs with two tiny green shoes which belong to a trapeze artist who is cut off by the picture frame.

## MYSTERY MAN

What many critics and art historians have tried to come to terms with is the strange perspective. The man reflected in the mirror should be standing in front of Suzon if the picture is to make sense. The bar is facing the spectator but the angle of the reflection is all wrong. The man is clearly 'missing' from the viewer's side of the bar unless Manet has made a fundamental mistake and he was too experienced an artist to have done so. The conclusion is that Manet has made a deliberate error but why?

## A BAR AT THE FOLIES BERGERE, 1881/82

Many different interpretations of this world famous painting exist. It is a quite straight-forward picture in some senses; Suzon, the barmaid, posed for Manet in the 'uniform' that she normally wore at work behind the bar. Behind her, reflected in the mirror, is depicted the balcony and audience of the Folies-Bergere along with chandeliers, Suzon's back and a male customer with top hat and cane in his left hand. She leans on the marble counter top which is ranged with bottles, a vase with roses and a crystal bowl holding tangerines.

## A MODERN VENUS

One view is that the barmaid is a modern day Venus, the goddess of love from classical antiquity. The writer Beth Archer Brombert points to the clues; in Suzon's dress and on the bar in front of Suzon is a white rose (symbol of purity) and a pink rose (symbol of divine love). The rose was commonly associated with Venus in Renaissance art, from which Manet often drew references, because the pricking of its thorns was compared to the wounds of love.

## A TRULY MODERN WOMA

When the painting was exhibited at the *Salon* the portrait of the barmaid received a mixed reaction. To one critic she had a *cardboard head*, to another *a beautiful girl, truly alive, truly modern*, and *the creature placed behind the bar... could not be more of a tart*. What is indisputable, however, is Suzon's complete detachment. She looks slightly down and to the lef of the viewer, avoiding eye contact, trapped betwe the spectator and the bar on one side and the cro and the male customer on the other. The painting seems to be about looking, about the male as a customer and the female as a commodity (a common interpretation is that Folies Bergere waitresses were often prostitutes) but also about painting; what is real and what is an illusion? Is this the reason for the 'missing' man? Has Manet cast us in his role?

# FAMOUS IMAGES

One of the best known of Manet's paintings is *A Bar at the Folies Bergere*. When he started the painting in 1881 his health was already failing and it was the last major work to be submitted to the *Salon*. In 1881 the Folies Bergere was a centre of entertainment which attracted a wide audience (it still offers nightly entertainment at 32 rue Richer). The venue was divided into a large hall with balconies and another large open area with bars. Its clientele comprised not only those interested in watching the events on stage but prostitutes and men of all classes on the look out for casual liaisons. Manet visited the bars and made sketches which were to be the basis of a studio painting. The barmaid, a model named Suzon, actually worked in the Folies-Bergere and was persuaded to pose for Manet behind a table in his studio.

## NIGHTLY ENTERTAINMENT

Every evening a range of activities could be found, including circus, cabaret, acrobats and dancers together with the offerings of a normal Parisian cafe.

## APPLE SUBSTITUTE?

Our attention is drawn to the tangerines on the counter in front of Suzon. Is Manet playing again with his art historical 'in jokes'? The orange (or tangerine) was sometimes used as a substitute for the apple from the Tree of Knowledge that Eve handed to Adam and so caused the fall from grace.

## MERY LAURENT, 1881/82

This detail from the reflection of the crowd on the balcony has been identified as a mini-portrait of Manet's friend, Mery Laurent. Mery Laurent started her career in Paris as a teenager working in cafe cabaret. She quickly attracted a following including many artists who were mesmerized by her beauty. She was supposed to have been the model for the central character in Emile Zola's novel *Nana* as well as having countless poems dedicated to her and portraits painted of her. It is likely that Manet was one of a string of lovers Mery Laurent is reported to have had among the literary and artistic set in Paris.

# THE AUDIENCE FOR THE PICTURES

*W*ho was Manet painting for? He was a man of independent financial means and therefore did not rely upon patrons or depend upon income from the sale of his paintings. What motivated Manet was the desire to be recognised as an artist. In Paris at the time that meant having work accepted by the *Salon* because there were only a few private galleries and these did not carry the same stamp of approval as the *Salon*. The problem was that Manet was so convinced that his way of painting was right that his pictures were continually refused by the *Salon*. In 1863 thousands of paintings were turned down by the *Salon* and a compromise was reached: a separate exhibition of refused paintings would be held at the same time. This separate exhibition, known as the *Salon des Refuses,* included Manet's Le *Dejeuner sur l'Herbe.*

### THE BATTLE OF THE KEARSAGE AND ALABAMA, 1864

When the American civil war reached as far as the French coast, all of France took notice. The sea battle off Cherbourg between the Unionist corvette *Kearsage* and the Confederate *Alabama* was a newsworthy event which Manet is reported to have witnessed at close hand. The painting was displayed in the window of a Paris art dealer where it attracted a great deal of attention, not all favourable. This was however, an opportunity for the public to view the event in an age before the widespread coverage of photography and film.

### THE ESCAPE OF ROCHEFORT, 1880/81

When Manet decided to paint a history painting (from the French, *histoire,* meaning story) about the escape of Henri Rochefort, he was effectively demonstrating to his audience his support for the Republic and his distaste for the Emperor. Rochefort had been a leading figure in the Communards and had been sentenced to life imprisonment in New Caledonia (an island in the Pacific). In 1874 he had made a dramatic escape and lived in Geneva until the French government amnesty of 1880. Rochefort himself supplied details of the escape for Manet to base the painting on. Rochefort and his supporters were enthusiastic about the picture but not surprisingly Manet decided against submitting it to the *Salon.*

A MEETING OF THE JUDGES OF THE SALON DES ARTISTES FRANCAIS, 1885 *Henri Gervex*

The procedure that decided which paintings were accepted was a long-standing one. A jury of 24 established academic painters, all men of course, stood in a group and voted paintings in (by raising a hand) or out. In 1867 Manet decided he could no longer bear the rejection of these conservative judges and planned his own exhibition. He borrowed 18,000 francs from his mother and built an exhibition space on the corner of Avenue Montaigne which housed 53 paintings. Manet's catalogue for the exhibition was prefaced with Reasons for a Private Exhibition. It went on to say '... *people have protested, because there is a traditional system of teaching... in painting, and because those who have been brought up according to such principles do not acknowledge any other... it is now only a question for the painter of gaining the goodwill of the public which has been turned into a would-be enemy'.*

## EMPEROR OF TASTE

It is said that when the *Salon* rejected so many paintings in 1863 the thousands of unhappy artists complained bitterly to the government. In desperation Emperor Napoleon was asked to intervene and he visited the *Salon* in person. Being unable to distinguish between those paintings that the jury had accepted and those they had refused, he ordered a separate exhibition to run alongside the official exhibition. This may not have pleased everyone, because many artists took offence and withdrew their paintings completely.

# WHAT THE CRITICS SAY

*M*anet wrote a letter to Baudelaire shortly after the opening of the 1865 *Salon* which exhibited his paintings of *Olympia* and *Jesus Mocked by Soldiers*. The letter began '*I wish I had you here, my dear Baudelaire, insults are beating down on me like hail, I've never been through anything like it... I wish I could have your sound judgement on my pictures because all this uproar is upsetting, and obviously something must be wrong.*' Manet was truly hurt by the torrent of abuse that followed the display of his work in the 1865 *Salon* and at other exhibitions. He wanted to be popular but his style of painting was always going to attract criticism. Baudelaire's reply was swift and harsh. Any true artist must not be concerned with the opinions of the critics and must have self belief. '*So I must speak to you of yourself,*' wrote Baudelaire '*I must try to show you what you are worth. What you demand is really stupid.*'

## SIR FREDERICK LEIGHTON

Leighton was an English artist and president of the Royal Academy of Art in London. His academy style was completely at odds with Manet's own. In 1878 Leighton visited Manet in his studio and commented on Manet's picture *The Skating Rink* saying '*It's very good but... don't you think the outlines are not well enough defined?*' Manet records that '*he realized he was annoying me and went away*'.
*Nausicaa (detail)*

## THE ARTIST'S CHAMPION

Charles Baudelaire was probably the most important figure in the development of Manet's art, and Manet looked continually to him for support. They had been friends since the 1850's and continued to be close until Baudelaire's death in 1867. Baudelaire was a 'modern' poet who sought 'modern beauty' in his poetry.

## PORTRAIT OF EMILE ZOLA, 1868

Zola was a great supporter of Manet and critic of the *Salon* system. He wrote for a weekly publication called *L'Evenement* which on 7 May 1866 included an article by Zola on Manet. He wrote '*It appears that I am the first to praise Manet without reservation. This is because I care little for all those boudoir paintings… those miserable canvases wherein I find nothing alive… I am so sure that Manet will be one of the masters of tomorrow that I should believe I had made a good bargain, had the money, in buying all his canvases today*'. Zola's view of the *Salon* jury was forthright: '*it hacks at art and offers the crowd only the mutilated corpse*'. It was with Zola's encouragement that Manet took the brave step of paying for a private exhibition of his work in 1867.

## THE ABUSED CRITIC

Jules Champfleury was a writer and critic and a good friend of Manet. Champfleury championed the Realist movement and was portrayed with Manet and other friends such as Baudelaire in Fantin-Latour's group portrait *Homage to Delacroix*. Champfleury was himself criticised for his association with the Realist artists and found himself caricatured in the popular press.

## MANET RIDICULED

The cover of this satirical paper dated 11 May 1876 shows a caricature of Edouard Manet, his head and hands poking through a hanging of paintings, presumably referring to the exhibition at the annual *Salon*. *L'Eclipse* ridiculed Manet in the 1860's when he submitted his paintings to the *Salon*, and a decade later it was still ridiculing him. An article of the time is to the point. '*It is true, entirely true, that Manet has almost unanimously been rejected…*' When the jury came to examine his paintings, one of the members exclaimed, '*Enough of this. We have allowed Manet ten years to turn over a new leaf. He hasn't done so… reject him!*'

## THE DUEL

Manet was in a furious mood after the critic Duranty had written a slightly critical appraisal of two of his paintings. He slapped Duranty on the face which was, as every gentleman knows, a challenge to a duel. The two men met in the forest of Saint Germain at 11am and fought with swords until Duranty was wounded. Fortunately the seconds declared honour was satisfied and the two men, rather relieved, made up.

# A LASTING IMPRESSION

**M**anet died on 30 April 1883 aged 51. He had been suffering for some time from the final stages of syphilis causing him constant pain and gangrene in his left foot, which was amputated 11 days before his death. Claude Monet, Antonin Proust, Emile Zola, Edgar Degas and Jacques-Emile Blanche all attended the funeral. Blanche is reported to have heard Degas say '*he was greater than we thought*'. This is a fitting epitaph for an artist whose influence on the course of nineteenth century art was profound. Today we first think of the Impressionists as the group who made the break from the traditional studio bound art of the time, but it was Manet who made it possible. He was the bridge between the old schools and the new. Manet's obsession with painting what he saw, the truth of the modern world, broke new ground for those who followed.

### THE FIGURE IN FOCUS

Manet made many full length studies of figures such as *The Tragic Actor, The Beggar, The Rag Picker* and *The Fifer*. His style, which was heavily criticised in his lifetime, was to portray the figure against a flat, neutral background. The figure appeared to be carefully, almost artificially, lit which had the effect of pushing it forward out of the background. His advice was '*In a figure, look for the full light and the full shadow, the rest will follow*'. In this detail from *The Fifer*, 1886 (shown here) Manet paints the boy in exactly this way with only a hint of shadow behind his feet to anchor him into the neutral background, which also serves to sharpen or 'focus' attention onto the figure.

### FASHION PHOTOGRAPHY

Manet's eye was very like the modern studio photographer's eye which also carefully arranges the lighting on the figure emphasising contrast and losing half tones. Today photographers make use of artificial backgrounds in exactly the way Manet did. The neutral flat backdrop serves to focus the viewer onto the subject and make the figure stand out.

## LE DEJEUNER SUR L'HERBE

*Pablo Picasso*

Manet's painting of the luncheon on the grass was like an earthquake in the art world; the aftershocks continued for many years. Picasso made this painting on the subject in 1960, nearly 100 years after Manet's version.

## BOW WOW WOW

The power of Manet's *Le Dejeuner sur l'Herbe* (left and on pages 14 & 15) has not been lost on those who followed. The allusions which were so full of scandalous meaning in Manet's time might not stir such emotions today but nevertheless the composition has been carefully copied for many different purposes. Even the latest versions present an image which seems to carry some promise of disrepute, as used on the cover of pop group Bow Wow Wow's record album *Go Wild in the Country*, 1981.

# GLOSSARY

**Engraving** - The word covers many different types of printing processes but should really only apply to the method of printing whereby lines are cut or etched into a metal plate and ink transferred from the grooves onto paper.

**Romanticism** - Romantic art was concerned with the expression of feelings and was at its height at the beginning of the 19th century, particularly with artists such as Delacroix.

**Tache** - A tache is a brushstroke which leaves a broad square or oblong stroke of paint on the canvas and is not smoothed into the surface of the canvas. Impressionists often painted quickly to give an effect or 'impression' of a scene and painted in large taches which are easily distinguishable as separate brushstrokes.

**Titian** - Titian was a 16th century Italian artist who is sometimes called the founder of modern painting. He painted in a very free style, using patches of colour, and sometimes putting the paint on with his fingers rather than a brush. The Impressionist style is often compared to his work.

**Values** - When applied to painting 'values' refer to the tonal graduations from light to dark. A 'tonal value' is a shade on that graduation which usually has to be translated into a colour equivalent unless the painting is monochrome.

**Venus** - The Roman goddess of love, identified with the Greek goddess Aphrodite, mother of Cupid. The portrayal of the female nude in art is often referred to as Venus without a particular link to the Roman myth.

## ACKNOWLEDGEMENTS

We would like to thank: Graham Rich, Tracey Pennington, and Peter Done for their assistance.
Copyright © 1997 ticktock Publishing Ltd., Great Britain.
First published in Great Britain by ticktock Publishing Ltd., Great Britain. All rights reserved.
No part of this publication may be reproduced, stored in a retrieval system, or transmitted in any form or by any means, electronic, mechanical, photocopying, recording or otherwise, without prior written permission of the copyright owner.

Acknowledgements: Picture Credits t=top, b=bottom, c=centre, l=left, r=right, OFC=outside front cover, IFC=inside front cover, IBC= inside back cover, OBC= outside back cover.

Photo © AKG London; 2/3cb, 4tl, OBC & 25tr. © BMG Entertainment International UK & Ireland; 31b. Copyright © British Museum; 15br. © Bibliothèque Nationale of France, Paris; 9t. Outfit by Caroline Charles, London; 30bl. Chateau de Compiegne, Oise/Lauros–Giraudon/Bridgeman Art Library, London; 17bl. Collections Royal Army Museum, Brussels; 16tl, OBC & 16cl. Courtauld Gallery, London/Bridgeman Art Library, London; 24. Mary Evans Picture Library; 3tl, 3tr, 4b, OBC & 29cl. Galleria degli Uffizi, Florence. Photo © AKG London; 18bl. Highgate Cemetery, London/Bridgeman Art Library, London; 2/3c. Kunsthalle, Hamburg. Photo © AKG London; 19tr. *Le Dejeuner sur L'Herbe*, 1960, Pablo Picasso © Succession Picasso/DACS 1997 (Private Collection. Photo © AKG London); 31t. *A Meeting of the Judges of the Salon des Artistes Francais*, 1885, Henri Gervex © ADAGP, Paris and DACS, London 1997 (Musee d'Orsay, Paris, France/Peter Willi/Bridgeman Art Library, London); 27t. Musee d'Orsay, Paris. Photo © AKG London; 5br, 26br. Musee d'Orsay, Paris. Photo © AKG London/Erich Lessing; 6cl & 28br & 29tr, 6bl, 8tl, 8/9c, 10tr, 11cr, 11br, 13bl & 18cr, OFCl & 21t, 29tl, OFCr & 30cl. Musee d'Orsay, Paris, France/Giraudon/Bridgeman Art Library, London; 6tr. Musee des Beaux-Arts, Nancy. Photo © AKG London; 25br. Musee du Louvre, Paris. Photo © AKG London; 7bl. Musee du Louvre, Paris. Photo © AKG London/Erich Lessing; IFC/1 & 13tl & 14/15c & 31cl. Museo del Prado, Madrid. Photo © AKG London/Erich Lessing; 16bl. Museum of Art, Philadelphia. Photo © AKG London; 26cl. Museum of Fine Arts, Boston, Massachusetts/Bridgeman Art Library, London; 12bl. *Gare Saint-Lazare*, Gift of Horace Havemeyer in memory of his mother, Louisine W. Havemeyer, © 1997 Board of Trustees, National Gallery of Art, Washington, 1873, oil on canvas, .933 x 1.115 (36 ¾ x 43 ¾); framed: 1.130 x 1.327 x .053 (44 ½ x 52 ¼ x 2 ⅛); 13cr and detail 13cl. National Gallery, London/Bridgeman Art Library, London; 22/23. National Maritime Museum, London; 3c. National Portrait Gallery, London. Photo © AKG London; 2bl. Neue Pinakothek, Munich. Photo © AKG London; 7tr. Städtische Kunsthalle, Mannheine, photo © AKG London/Erich Lessing; OBC & 16/17ct. Private Collection. Photo © AKG London; 28l. Private Collection/Giraudon/Bridgeman Art Library, London; OBC & 11cl. Pushkin Museum, Moscow. Photo © AKG London; 8bl. The Royal Collection, London. Photo © AKG London; 27br. Szepmueveszeti Muzeum, Budapest. Photo © AKG London; 5tl.

Every effort has been made to trace the copyright holders and we apologise in advance for any unintentional omissions. We would be pleased to insert the appropriate acknowledgement in any subsequent edition of this publication.

A CIP Catalogue for this book is available from the British Library. ISBN 1 86007 055 8

snapping-turtle
guide